21st CENTURY CITIZEN
Animal Rights

Kay Woodward

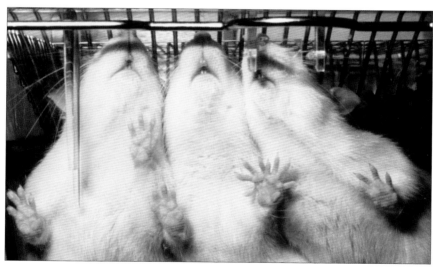

FRANKLIN
WATTS

First published in 2004, reprinted in 2005 by
Franklin Watts
96 Leonard Street
London EC2A 4XD

Franklin Watts Australia
45-51 Huntley Street
Alexandria NSW 2015

Produced by Arcturus Publishing Limited,
26/27 Bickels Yard, 151-153 Bermondsey Street, London SE1 3HA

© 2004 Arcturus Publishing Limited

Series concept: Alex Woolf
Editor: Kelly Davis
Designer: Stonecastle Graphics
Consultant: Michaela Miller
Picture researcher: Shelley Noronha, Glass Onion Pictures

Picture acknowledgements
Popperfoto 8 (Regis Duvignau), 10 (Russell Boyce), 23 (Anthony P. Bolante), 24 (Peter Macdiarmid),
30 (Enny Nuraheni), 32 (Sergei Teterin), 33 (Will Burgess), 38 (Claudia Daut), 41 (Duncan Willetts),
44 (Hyungwon Kang); RSPCA 6 (Tom Claxton), 11 (Dr Matt Ruglys), 12 (Colin Seddon), 29, 31 (Robin Culley),
36 (Niva G Images); RSPCA/Angela Hampton 7, 28; Rex Features 19 and cover (below);
Science Photo Library 1 and 20 (Klaus Guldbrandsen), 26; Topham 5 (Nancy Richmond), 14, 16 and cover (top),
17 (EMPICS), 21 (Fritz Hoffmann), 25 (John Griffin), 34 (The British Library), 37 (Laurie Lewis/PAL),
39 (David Jennings), 40 (Charles Walker), 42, 43 (Polfoto).
**Cover pictures: After a morning of hunting, two men load a young deer into a pick-up truck in Texas, USA (above). Caged
protesters campaign to raise awareness of the suffering of animals on fur farms, at an animal rights demonstration in
Helsinki, Finland (below).**

British Library Cataloguing Publication Data
A CIP catalogue record for this book is available from the British Library.

ISBN 0 7496 5462 7

Printed and bound in Thailand

Note to parents and teachers
Some recommended websites are listed under 'Useful Addresses' at the back of this book. Every effort has been
made by the Publishers to ensure that these websites are suitable for children; that they are of the highest
educational value; and that they contain no inappropriate or offensive material. However, because of the nature of
the Internet, it is impossible to guarantee that the content of these sites will not be altered. We strongly advise that
Internet access is supervised by a responsible adult.

Contents

1 **What are Animal Rights?**   4

2 **Farming**   6

3 **Hunting**   14

4 **Animal Research**   20

5 **Pets**   28

6 **Animal Entertainment**   34

7 **Endangered Species**   40

Glossary   46

Useful Addresses   47

Further Reading   47

Index   48

1: What are Animal Rights?

Do animals have the right to be treated in exactly the same way as humans? Should humans be allowed to use animals in experiments – as long as the animals do not suffer? Should deer be hunted? Does a dolphin have more right to live than an insect? What are animal rights?

Humans and animals

There is no simple definition of 'animal rights'. Some people believe that animals have exactly the same rights as humans. They argue that humans are no more important than animals, that humans should not use animals – in farming, as pets or in experiments – and that animals have the right to be free. These people are often said to believe in animal rights.

However, other people believe that humans should be able to farm animals, keep them as pets and experiment on them, but that these animals should be looked after, treated with respect, and not subjected to unnecessary pain. This is called believing in animal welfare.

The animal rights movement

Although concerns about the welfare of animals were first voiced in nineteenth-century England, it was not until 1975 – when philosophers such as Peter Singer, Richard Ryder and Tom Regan began to raise questions about animals' rights – that the animal rights movement really gained support. Singer argued

PERSPECTIVES

The FAWC (Farm Animal Welfare Council) in the UK lists the 'five freedoms' below as guidelines for acceptable animal welfare. Taken together, they provide a good definition of the basic rights many people believe animals should have.

1. Freedom from hunger and thirst.
2. Freedom from discomfort.
3. Freedom from pain, injury or disease.
4. Freedom to behave normally.
5. Freedom from fear and distress.

PERSPECTIVES

Peter Singer, an Australian philosopher, made comments in his 1975 book *Animal Liberation* that are considered by many people to have begun the modern animal rights movement.

'Speciesism … is a prejudice … in favour of the interests of members of one's own species and against those of members of another species. It should be obvious that the fundamental objections to racism and sexism … apply equally to speciesism. If possessing a higher degree of intelligence does not entitle one human to use another for his or her own ends, how can it entitle humans to exploit nonhumans for the same purpose?'

that the fact that animals are less intelligent than humans does not mean that they should be exploited and their feelings disregarded. Ryder went on to liken speciesism – discrimination against other species – to sexism and racism.

Since the 1970s, countless organizations and groups around the world have voiced their opinions on the rights of animals. This remains a very hotly debated topic.

A flock of sheep in Durango, Colorado, USA, on a three-day walk from their winter home to their spring home. Do they have the right to freedom from hunger, thirst, pain, discomfort and fear?

DEBATE

Should animals and humans have the same rights?

2: Farming

Farm animals are bred and reared in order to provide humans with products such as meat, eggs, milk, butter, cheese and leather. Cattle, sheep, pigs, goats, horses, donkeys, mules, buffalo, oxen and camels are just a few of the animals that are farmed around the world.

Some animal rights' groups are against farming, because all farm animals have a shorter lifespan than they would naturally enjoy. Other groups see the animals' welfare as the biggest concern – they are keen to ensure that farm animals are well treated.

Broilers and laying hens

Chickens are among the animals that receive the most publicity from welfare groups. They are bred in two different ways. Broilers are chickens – both male and female – that are bred just for their meat. Laying hens are female chickens that are bred to produce eggs for human consumption.

Most broilers spend their short lives in large sheds, with no access to outside space. Their ancestors had a lifespan of seven to nine years, but farmed broilers are slaughtered when they are only about six weeks old. (Their carefully balanced diet, containing protein, minerals, vitamins and antibiotics, makes them grow to adult size very quickly.)

Battery hens living in cramped conditions.

Laying hens each lay around 300 eggs a year. In Europe, they are killed for meat at 12 to 18 months, because they start to lay fewer eggs after this time. Over 90 per cent of laying hens are kept in battery cages, which are very cramped. These cages are so small that the birds have no room even to flap their wings. Many also have problems with their feet, because of the wire floor. In the USA, some laying hens live for up to 32 months, although the majority of all hens still spend their time in battery cages.

Animal welfare groups have long campaigned for improved conditions for farmed chickens. Their efforts have led to better living conditions for a small percentage of broilers and laying hens. Free-range broilers and laying hens may have more room to move around and access to outside space. They may not be bred to grow as quickly as other chickens. Organic broilers are also free to roam, but are fed organic food too.

Free-range and organic chickens and their eggs are labelled to show consumers that the produce has been reared in a more humane way. Many people also believe that free-range and organic food is tastier. However, labels such as 'farm fresh' simply mean that the eggs come from farms and were probably laid by hens in battery cages. Products such as ready meals and cakes are usually made with battery eggs, although some major supermarkets and restaurant chains have now pledged that all eggs in their pre-prepared meals will be from free-range hens. Conventional battery cages are to be banned in Europe in 2012.

Free-range hens roaming in a field.

Cattle

There are two types of cattle – dairy and beef. On average, a dairy cow will produce over 23 litres of milk a day. A cow's milk is used to make other dairy products, such as cream, cheese and yoghurt. In order to continue producing milk, each dairy cow gives birth to one calf a year. These calves either grow up to become dairy or beef cattle, or are slaughtered when they are very young for their tender meat. Although cattle have a natural lifespan of 20 to 30 years, dairy cows are usually slaughtered when they are five years old (because they are worn out from producing so many offspring and so much milk) and sold for meat.

Beef cattle are bred just for their meat, which is also sold as steak, mince and sausages. They roam outdoors for part of their lives and are slaughtered when they are about 18 months old – when the meat is at its best.

In some parts of the world, female cattle are allowed total freedom. In India, for instance, cows are greatly respected (according to the Hindu religion) and are allowed to roam wherever they like. The slaughter of milk-producing cows is strictly forbidden.

Veal and foie gras

There are some types of meat that even many meat eaters refuse to eat, on the grounds that the animals are treated in a totally unacceptable way. Veal and foie gras are among these controversial foodstuffs.

Veal is the meat that comes from dairy calves. The calves are fed a special diet of milk and high-protein calf meal, before being slaughtered as little as three weeks after their birth. Veal has a low fat content and pale colour and is seen as a delicacy by many. Veal crates – wooden boxes where calves are kept for the whole of their short lives – have now been banned in the UK. Campaigners hope to stop the practice in other countries.

A French chef works near trays holding traditional luxury foie gras from duck livers. Ducks and geese are force-fed corn for more than a month to produce the livers, which weigh 500–600 g.

Pâté de foie gras is a smooth, rich paste made from the liver of a goose or duck that has been fattened by force-feeding. Most of the birds are kept in small cages and are fed until their liver is ten times its normal size, causing problems with breathing and walking. About 90 per cent of foie gras is made and eaten in France. Some other countries have banned its production, but still import the delicacy. Campaigners would like to see a total ban.

Intensive farming

Factory farms are designed to raise a great many animals in a very small space, and make as much money as possible. These enormous, largely automated enterprises are said to have driven millions of small family farms out of business since 1945 – three million in the US alone.

Some agricultural experts claim that intensive farming methods (particularly the use of ground-up animal carcasses in animal feed) have led to the spread of diseases that are harmful to animals (such as foot-and-mouth disease) and, in some cases, to humans. For example, BSE (bovine spongiform encephalopathy), also known as 'mad cow disease', has been linked with CJD (Creutzfeldt-Jakob disease) in humans. Both BSE and CJD are fatal. Organic farming, a return to animal breeding and crop-growing without the use of chemicals, is becoming increasingly widespread. Organically produced meat is usually more expensive, but the consumer can be confident that the animal has been bred in a more natural way. However this type of farming is also less cost-effective and so consumers usually have to pay more for organic products.

PERSPECTIVES

The Organic Farming Research Foundation in California, USA, is optimistic about the future of organic farming.

'As the public becomes increasingly concerned about the negative effects of industrial agriculture on the environment and on their bodies, the demand for safe food is skyrocketing. Organic agriculture offers a bright light in the troubled future of family farming, providing small farms with an economically and environmentally healthy alternative for their survival.'

The Organic Farming Research Foundation website, June 2003

Animal transportation

There has been a lot of controversy about the way in which animals are taken to market or to new owners. In the past, truckloads of livestock have been transported great distances, spending many hours in very cramped conditions without food and water. Laws in the UK now limit the length of time that animals can go without food and water to 15 hours. Campaigners are hoping to get the maximum journey time reduced still further. It is hoped that other countries will soon follow this lead.

Fishing

Since prehistoric times, humans have fished in order to feed themselves. Until relatively recently, the amount of fishing carried out in the seas, rivers and lakes of the world was not

Sheep being transported in Europe in 1995.

large enough to have a great impact on the numbers and species of sea creatures. However, engines and powered lifting gear were introduced in the fishing industry towards the end of the nineteenth century, followed by technological improvements during the twentieth century, which led to a huge increase in the numbers of fish caught.

In the past, it was believed by many that, unlike humans and animals, fish did not feel pain (which is one of the reasons why some people eat fish, but not meat). However, in 2003, the results of experiments on trout suggested that fish do feel pain after all. This may affect the ways in which fish are caught and killed in the future, in order to avoid unnecessary suffering.

A harbour (or common) porpoise drowned after being caught in a fishing net.

Drift nets are large fishing nets that have weights at the bottom and floats at the top, enabling them to drift through the sea, catching fish such as tuna and sea bass as they go. Unfortunately, these nets also catch other sea creatures, such as dolphins and

CASE STUDY

Overfishing and loss of habitat are two of the factors that are said to have led to the decline of wild salmon around the world. As demand for salmon is increasing, the fish are being farmed instead, leading to concerns about their welfare.

In 2002, Loch Duart in Scotland became the first fish farm to be awarded the RSPCA's Freedom Food certification for farmed salmon. The farm aims to give its fish a good life, while having no impact on the environment. A fish welfare officer monitors the salmon to ensure that they have adequate rest breaks and that their feeding is controlled. There are also strict limits on the number of times the salmon are handled.

Managing Director Nick Joy says, 'We have always regarded the welfare of our fish as extremely important. It also means that our customers receive a better tasting, better looking fish.'

Sales Director Andrew Bing adds, 'For our customers, Freedom Food is a label that means caring and responsible farming. We know this produces the best salmon both in appearance and taste. To consumers who care about the quality of life of farmed animals, this is an important endorsement.'

A salmon farm in the Shetland Islands.

PERSPECTIVES

The Vegetarian Society has been promoting vegetarianism since 1847.

'The Vegetarian Society defines a vegetarian as a person who eats no meat, poultry, game, fish, shellfish or crustacea. Vegetarians also avoid the by-products of slaughter such as gelatine or animal rennet in cheese. The Society only approves products containing eggs when they are free-range... Vegetarianism is growing and becoming more mainstream, but vegetarians are still only a small proportion of the [UK] population... We've come a long way, but we're not satisfied – there's still a lot of work to be done.'

porpoises. Although the International Dolphin Conservation Act of 1992 called for the end of large-scale drift net fishing, several countries still use this method. Animal rights and welfare organizations around the world are seeking to end this practice.

Vegetarianism

A vegetarian is someone who eats no meat. About a quarter of the world's population lives on a mainly vegetarian diet, for moral, religious or health reasons. In Europe and the USA, the proportion is much smaller, although vegetarian groups claim that more people are opting for a meat-free diet. Others extend or limit the range of food they eat, leading to different types of vegetarianism.

• Vegetarians do not eat meat – flesh, fish or fowl.
• Piscatarians do not eat meat, but eat fish and seafood.
• Vegans do not eat or use any animal products. They also refuse to use products that are made using animals, such as leather shoes.

DEBATE

There are many arguments against the farming of animals – whether this is carried out in a humane or inhumane way. However, it is worth considering the future of farm animals if the whole world were to turn vegetarian. Where would they live? Would they be able to survive in the wild? If not, would they be left to die out?

3: Hunting

Chasing and killing wild animals or game is known as hunting. There are three main types of hunting – hunting for sport, hunting for food, and hunting to control animal numbers – although people often hunt for more than one of these reasons. Those who take part in these activities feel that their actions are justifiable, but many animal lovers feel strongly that hunting should be banned altogether.

The history of hunting

In the past, people hunted in order to survive. After an animal was killed, its meat was eaten, its skin was worn and its bones were used to make tools – nothing was wasted. As time went on, people increasingly turned towards agriculture, which provided other sources of food. They still hunted for food but now they also farmed animals and grew crops.

A medieval stag hunt with hounds.

PERSPECTIVES

Founded in 1957, Friends of Animals is an American activist group that works to protect animals from cruelty and abuse.

'Friends of Animals opposes hunting. All hunting. The more we study the excuses offered by hunters, the more we see they are baseless. Friends of Animals holds that hunting is ethically wrong – it imposes capital punishment on innocent animals essentially for the amusement or "recreation" of someone who enjoys killing. Friends of Animals has determined that hunting is ecologically disruptive, and ... considers hunting to be sociologically disreputable.'

Then, around the seventh century BC, a new reason for hunting developed. Rulers and nobles began hunting for sport. The idea of keeping game, such as deer or pheasants, in order to hunt them, was firmly established by the seventeenth century, when hunting was linked with owning land. Hunting with guns had also been introduced by this time. Now it was easier for hunters to kill their quarry from further away.

Hunting as a sport still exists, but many groups campaign against it. Today, few people hunt animals in order to survive. As the world's many vegetarians have proved, it is possible to live without meat.

PERSPECTIVES

The International Fund for Animal Welfare campaigns against the seal hunting that takes place in Newfoundland each year. They would like to see the practice banned.

'Seal pups have traditionally been clubbed to death, but in recent years thinning ice has led to increased shooting on ice and in open water. When clubbing, sealers may only "stun" a pup, resulting in the skinning or bleeding of a live seal. Shooting also causes significant suffering. The Royal Commission on Seals and Sealing recognized it is extremely difficult to guarantee a clean kill when shooting at seals in the water or on moving ice floes. Seals are often wounded and escape to die under the ice.'

The International Fund for Animal Welfare website, July 2003

Culling or sport?

People have different reasons for hunting animals. Some say they love the thrill of the chase, others like the skill involved in shooting a moving target, and others hunt in order to cull (reduce the population of a species).

In the USA, deer are hunted for their meat – called venison – and hides, which are made into leather. Their antlers are sometimes kept as trophies. Deer hunting is a controversial sport. The country's deer population used to be controlled by coyotes, wolves and mountain lions – the deer's natural predators. Now that many of these predators have disappeared, deer are able to breed freely.

After a morning of hunting, two men load a young deer into a pick-up truck in Texas, USA.

Some sport deer hunters in the USA argue that hunting is humane because, if deer herds were allowed to grow too big, there would not be enough food to go round and the animals would starve to death. Many say that deer would go on to destroy farmers' crops in search of food. These hunters argue that they are merely helping to maintain an environmental balance.

Those who hunt with dogs claim that fox hunting, hare hunting, deer hunting and mink hunting prevent their quarry from becoming pests. They say that if hunting with dogs were banned, many people – such as farriers and grooms – would be unemployed and that the dogs themselves might have to be put down.

Humane alternatives to hunting

Although most animal rights supporters feel that it is wrong to kill animals for sport, or even to cull them, many accept that, in some cases, numbers do need to be reduced. Humane ways of culling a species include: sterilizing animals so that they cannot

Clay-pigeon shooting.

continue to breed; and encouraging birds to lay eggs in artificial nests, so that the eggs can easily be removed and destroyed. Traps have also been developed to catch, rather than kill, mice and other small rodents. The animals can then be released – unharmed. This will not cut the numbers of a species, but will control a pest problem.

Meanwhile, new humane activities have been developed to take the place of bloodsports. With clay-pigeon shooting, a saucer-shaped piece of baked clay is fired up into the air, forming the target. The object of the sport is to shoot at and hit as many clay pigeons as possible.

PERSPECTIVES

Support Fox Hunting is a group that is opposed to a proposed ban on hunting with dogs in the UK.

'Fox hunting with dogs is an age-old sport, a British tradition and a major part of the British countryside. Banning fox hunting will only add to problems in the countryside and will be the start of the end for country sports, with fishing and shooting already under threat.'

The Support Fox Hunting website, June 2003

Drag hunting is another humane sport that is growing in popularity. Instead of dogs, horses and riders chasing a fox, the hunt follows a trail laid by a human. A person walks across the countryside, dragging a piece of heavy material that has been soaked in a strong-smelling substance, such as paraffin, aniseed or animal dung. When the dogs are released, they pick up the scent and lead the hunt along the trail. As an animal's primary concern is escaping from the hunt, rather than laying an exciting trail, many riders prefer following an artificial scent to animal scent. With drag hunting, they are guaranteed a variety of terrain, with plenty of galloping and jumping.

Poaching

Laws govern when and where animals can be hunted. When people illegally hunt or catch game or fish on someone else's land, or when there are laws protecting the animal concerned, this is known as poaching. Poachers usually hunt because the animal, or some part of it, can be sold for a large sum of money.

For example, the high price of ivory means that elephants have been hunted for their tusks for many years in African countries. There are now laws to prevent this happening, and park rangers protect elephants from poachers who ignore the laws. Piano keys and white billiard balls – once made of ivory – are now made from synthetic materials.

The fur debate

Perhaps the most controversial area of hunting concerns the fur industry. When people first hunted, the most important part of

CASE STUDY

In Eastern Africa, in May 2002, a female elephant was shot and killed by poachers, but her six-month-old calf escaped. By the time the baby elephant was discovered by a herdsman, it was thirsty, hungry and very thin. The herdsman arranged for the elephant to be taken to the David Sheldrick Wildlife Trust, near Nairobi, Kenya, where it could be properly cared for. There, the young elephant was nursed back to full health. Named Mpala, after the area in which it was found, the elephant is now safe, well, and protected from danger.

The David Sheldrick Wildlife Trust website

an animal was its meat. Its fur was a by-product that was used to make warm clothes. However, by the time of early North American settlers, fur had become big business.

Animals such as mink, fox and chinchilla are now raised on farms for their fur, often suffering in the heat in the summer months, while raccoon, beaver and skunk are caught in traps. In the twenty-first century, many animal rights groups have criticized both the hunting and farming of animals for fur. Activists have even splashed fur-wearers with paint to make their feelings clear.

Caged protesters campaign to raise awareness of the suffering of animals on fur farms, at an animal rights demonstration in Helsinki, Finland.

DEBATE

Throughout the world's food chain, many animals hunt, kill and eat other animals. If animals hunt animals, why shouldn't humans hunt animals?

4: Animal Research

Animal research takes place for three main reasons: to find out how animals' bodies work, in order to improve the health of both humans and animals; to make sure that chemicals are safe for humans to use; and to educate students.

The history of animal research

Animal experiments first took place in ancient Greece, over two thousand years ago, when scientists cut open live pigs in order to find out how their bodies functioned. Experiments continued in the Middle Ages, with early surgeons also practising their skills on animals before carrying out operations on humans.

By the nineteenth century, animal research had become much more common – and opposition to it had grown. Animal research continued to grow steadily until the 1950s, when there was a huge increase in the number of experiments carried out on animals to test consumer products (such as detergents and cosmetics) and drugs.

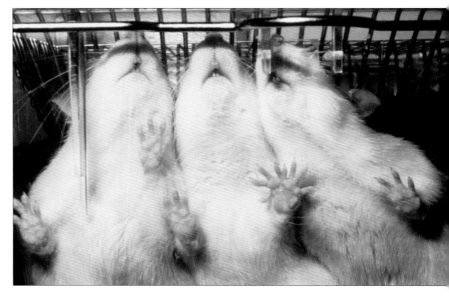

The growing power of the animal rights movement and concerns about animal welfare now mean that there are greater controls over the use of animals in science. In many countries, animal researchers have to have a licence. In addition, before any experiment can take place, it too has to be approved and licensed to ensure that it will be carried out properly, that animals will be well treated and that the benefits of the experiment justify the cost to the animals concerned.

Millions of animals still die in experiments every year but now, in the twenty-first century, there is a much greater emphasis on the search for alternatives to animal research. Many hope that there will come a time when animals are no longer involved in this area of science.

Three laboratory mice in a cage. Mice are the most commonly used animals for research to test the safety of cosmetics and pesticides and for medical experiments to test the effect of new drugs. Although animal experiments are controversial, and alternatives are being developed, many of these experiments remain compulsory by law before new products can be released.

Arguments for and against animal research

Should animals be used in experiments? This question tends to provoke a variety of responses – some positive, some negative and some extreme. Many people feel that animal research is justified, but only in certain circumstances.

Those who support animal research argue that it is the best way of developing vaccines and medicines for humans. One reason they give for this is that animals' and humans' bodies are alike, and that they suffer from similar illnesses and diseases. This means that animals react to tests in a similar way to humans. In addition, as animals have shorter life cycles than humans, it takes less time to study them from birth to death.

One of the most convincing arguments in favour of animal research is the enormous list of medical advances that have been achieved because of the use of animals in the laboratory. These include: antibiotics; vaccines for diphtheria, measles, polio, smallpox and tetanus; insulin – used to control diabetes; chemotherapy for cancer patients; pacemakers – used to help those with heart problems; the discovery of the HIV virus; drugs to treat AIDS; and techniques for transplanting organs.

A child being vaccinated in Nashville, Tennessee, USA. Vaccinations against diseases like smallpox and measles have helped save millions of people from disability and death.

PERSPECTIVES

Americans for Medical Progress (AMP) is in favour of animal research.

'Virtually all medical advances and discoveries of the past [twentieth] century were based in animal research. Some examples include vaccines for diseases like smallpox and polio, as well as anaesthesia, aspirin and insulin... If we were to abolish the use of live animals entirely, we would be unable to investigate the effects of how one system (for example, the nervous system) interacts with another (for example, the immune system...), while monitoring side effects (effects on respiration, kidney function or heart rate).'

The Americans for Medical Progress website, June 2003

Those who disagree with animal research argue that animals have the right to live and that humans do not have the right to carry out experiments on them for human needs. Many animal rights supporters argue that humans should be used in experiments instead of animals. It has been suggested that results from animal research do not necessarily apply to humans. For example, vivisection groups claim that although penicillin acts as an antibiotic to humans, it causes death to guinea pigs.

There is very strong opposition to experiments carried out on animals in order to test non-essential products such as soap, toothpaste, face cream, make-up and hairspray. Even though it is claimed that many products sold today have not been tested on animals, the majority of cosmetics contain ingredients that have gone through animal testing in the past.

Most people find it difficult to decide whether they agree or disagree with animal research. However, many feel that animals should not be used to test cosmetics, while believing that animal research carried out with the purpose of developing cures for deadly diseases is acceptable.

Genetic engineering

Each living creature carries genes inside its body that carry information about it. For instance, genes passed from parents to their offspring define how they will look, grow and behave, and whether or not they will develop certain diseases during their lifetime. Genetic engineering aims to change living beings, either by altering their genes or by moving genes from one living being to another.

Many animals used in research are used for genetic modification – over half a million a year in the UK alone. Worldwide, millions of animals are genetically modified every year – for many reasons. Genetic engineering of animals:

• enables researchers to find out more about what genes do, and how they behave

• helps researchers to breed farm animals that grow faster or produce more meat

• can help reduce disease in animals

• produces animals that can be used to treat human diseases, and animals whose organs can be used for human transplant.

Many people who are against genetic engineering believe that humans do not have the right to change animals for their own purposes. They are opposed to any suffering and death that may happen during these experiments. There is also concern about what will happen when genetically modified animals come into contact with wild animals and perhaps interbreed with them.

The world's first successfully cloned mule, in May 2003. Scientists in Idaho, USA, had been working on the project, which involved complex genetic engineering techniques, since 1998.

PERSPECTIVES

'If abandoning animal research means that there are some things we cannot learn, then so be it... We have no basic right ... not to be harmed by those natural diseases we are heir to.'

Tom Regan, The Case for Animal Rights *(Routledge, 1983)*

Vivisection

The practice of performing operations on live animals for the purpose of scientific research is known as vivisection. Some people feel so strongly about vivisection and other types of animal research that they will go to great lengths to stop these experiments taking place. Animal liberation groups have protested outside research laboratories and even freed the animals inside. And some animal rights supporters have been known to resort to violence to get their message across. Also known as eco-terrorists, these extreme animal rights activists have attacked shops that sell fur products and bombed laboratories that perform experiments on animals. However, the vast majority of opponents to vivisection rely on peaceful protest to try to persuade researchers to stop using live animals in experiments.

An animal rights protester calls for the closure of Huntingdon Life Sciences (a laboratory known to use animals for research), near Cambridge, UK, in July 2002.

PERSPECTIVES

Anti Vivisection WA (Inc), based in Western Australia, is against animal research.

'Animal experiments are poorly suited to addressing the urgent health problems of our era, such as … heart disease, cancer, stroke, AIDS and birth defects. The majority of animals in laboratories are used as so-called animal models… researchers try to produce ailments in these animals that 'model' human conditions. However, the innumerable subtle, but significant, differences between species severely undermines the extrapolation [transferring] of animal data to other species, including humans, and delivers often dangerously misleading results.'

The Anti Vivisection WA (inc) website, June 2003

Benefits for animals

Experiments carried out on animals have not just benefited humans – many have helped other animals to live longer, healthier lives. Medicines and vaccines developed for use on humans are now also used to treat and heal animals. These include vaccines for rabies and distemper (diseases that affect dogs and other animals) and

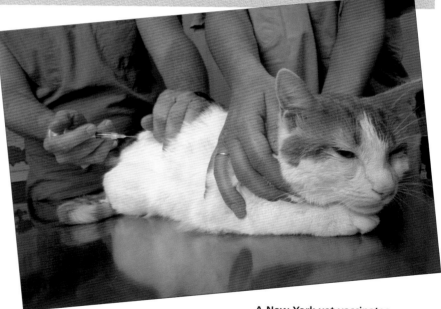

A New York vet vaccinates a cat against rabies.

PERSPECTIVES

'It is not only humans who benefit from medical research: all animals within our care have an interest in it, and the assumption must be that it is so conducted that the long-term benefits to all of us, human and animal, outweigh the short-term costs in pain and discomfort.'

Roger Scruton, Animal Rights and Wrongs *(Metro Books, 2000)*

treatment to prevent tuberculosis in cattle. Those in favour of animal research also claim that experiments have helped many endangered species to survive, by solving problems with breeding, feeding and pollution problems caused by a changing environment.

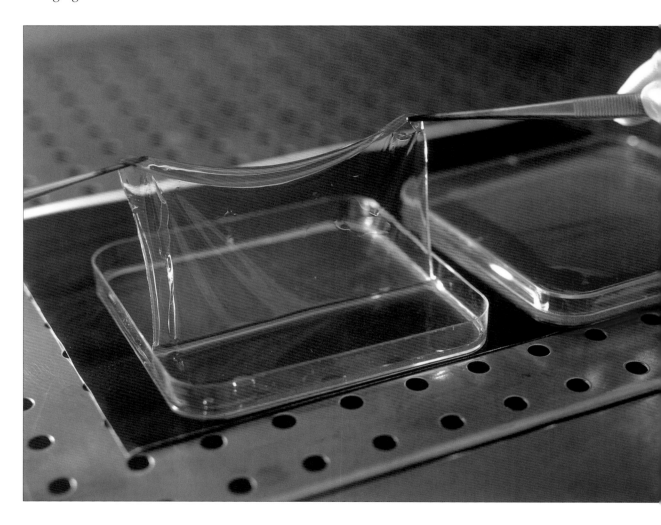

Alternatives to animal research

In 1959, British researchers Russell and Burch introduced three ways of reducing or preventing animal suffering. Known as 'the three Rs', these are replacement, reduction and refinement.

Replacement involves replacing animal experiments with ones that do not involve live animals, such as experiments using humans or using cells and tissues grown in laboratories. For example, Corrositex is a revolutionary type of man-made skin that can be used in experiments instead of real, living skin.

Artificially grown skin being removed from a culture dish in order to make a skin graft. It can be used to help restore skin to victims of serious burns. It can also be used for some research experiments, thereby avoiding the use of animals.

CASE STUDY

The LD50 test was an animal experiment that was developed in 1927. LD50 stands for 'lethal dose to 50 per cent'. It involved testing a group of animals by force-feeding them larger and larger amounts of a particular chemical until 50 per cent of the animals died. This experiment was condemned by animal rights supporters around the world on the grounds that it caused enormous suffering. Others questioned whether the test actually worked at all, as different results could be achieved in the same laboratory using the same doses. As a result of animal rights groups' continued protests, the test was banned by the Organization for Economic Cooperation and Development (OECD) in December 2002. (The OECD administers an international test guidelines programme agreed by its 30 member countries, including the United States.)

In medical and veterinary colleges, interactive computer programs and videos are increasingly being used to demonstrate dissection and veterinary techniques. In these situations, it is no longer necessary to use animals.

Reduction means reducing the number of animals used in a particular experiment. Computer programs have been developed that are capable of looking at research information in a much more in-depth way. This means that fewer tests need to be carried out in order to get results. Also, if researchers are studying different parts of an animal, they might both experiment on the same animal, meaning that fewer animals are used.

Finally, refinement means altering experiments so that animals' suffering is lessened. More effective use of painkillers, improved living conditions and better handling techniques can all help. Modern medical techniques, such as ultrasound scanning, can be used to look inside an animal, without the need for operating. The use of experiments that do not end in the animals' death is perhaps the best type of refinement.

DEBATE

Many small mammals – including rats, mice, rabbits and guinea pigs – are bred specifically for animal research. Is human benefit more important than the suffering these animals may undergo? Are there instances when animal research is acceptable? Where should animal researchers draw the line?

5: Pets

Owning a pet is a huge responsibility. All pets need to be cared for, and different pets have different needs. For instance, dogs need to be taken for daily walks; cats need access to outside space; and rabbits need the company of other rabbits.

The history of pets

Pets are animals that people keep to enjoy their company. Many of the most popular pets – such as cats and dogs – are domesticated. This means that they are tame and have been brought up to behave in a particular way. (Wild animals act as they like, and live where they like, without human interference.)

A young girl with her hamster. For city-dwellers without big gardens, hamsters are easier to look after than dogs and cats.

The first animal to become a pet was tamed thousands of years ago and was probably a dog. In ancient Egyptian times, small dogs were pampered, while greyhounds hunted with their owners. The ancient Egyptians also tamed lions, hyenas and monkeys.

However, the ancient Egyptians' most popular pet was the cat, which was said to be sacred. Cats were actually worshipped in temples!

Throughout history, pets have had their own roles, such as

PERSPECTIVES

Brian Kilcommons has owned and trained dogs for many years. 'With their unquestioning devotion comes obligation. Caring for a dog is a commitment… We owe them our highest selves, not our upset, anger or impatience. Why a dog? In short, to love and be loved.'

Brian Kilcommons and Sarah Wilson, Good owners, great dogs *(Warner Books, 1999)*

CASE STUDY

Every year, animal protection charities all over the world help many thousands of animals that are neglected, treated badly or in danger. Peanut, a Jack Russell terrier, was rescued in the UK by the Royal Society for the Prevention of Cruelty to Animals (RSPCA).

Peanut was just eight months old when an RSPCA inspector found him, covered in fleas and sores, cowering in a ferret cage. The Jack Russell was suffering from mange (sore, ulcerated skin) and significant hair loss. He also had overgrown claws. As the RSPCA inspector attempted to take Peanut away, the dog's owner stopped her. He offered to shoot the Jack Russell to put it out of its misery. Of course, the inspector declined this offer.

In August 2002, a court found Peanut's owner guilty of causing unnecessary suffering to the dog by failing to get veterinary treatment. Although he was not jailed, the man was fined.

Fortunately, Peanut made a full recovery and found a loving new home. His was just one of many stories highlighted by the RSPCA in their 2002 campaign against cruelty to animals.

Peanut, just one of the many animals rescued by the RSPCA.

hunting, guarding or herding other animals, protecting property-owners, or catching mice, rats and other pests. Over the last few decades, pets have become enormously popular. They are now at the centre of a huge industry that employs millions of people worldwide. Pet shops sell animals and pet accessories. Pet-sitters look after pets when their owners are away. Pet-trainers teach animals to obey commands. Dog-walkers exercise pets if their owners are too busy. Pet-groomers brush and clean pets to keep them looking their best. Vets give animals – including pets – medical treatment. There are even pet cemeteries. Finally, and most importantly, animal welfare organizations exist to ensure that animals are well looked after.

A new pet

Pets can be bought from pet shops or breeders, adopted from rescue centres, or (in the case of goldfish) won at fairgrounds – a practice which many animal lovers are against.

Specialist breeders rear certain types of pet, such as poodles or Siamese cats. If people know exactly which breed of animal they want to buy, this is often the best place to find their new pet.

Unwanted, neglected or homeless pets are kept at rescue centres until new owners can be found for them. These centres look after all sorts of pets, including cats, dogs, hamsters, rabbits and even horses. Anyone wishing to adopt a pet has to answer a series of questions, such as:

Goldfish on sale in Jakarta, Indonesia.

- Why do you want an animal?
- Where will the animal be kept?
- Is your house suitable?
- What other animals live in the house?
- Will the animal be left alone at any time during the day?

The answers to these questions will help those at rescue centres to decide whether people are able to give animals the care and attention they need. Their homes may be checked, to make sure that they are suitable for the animals to live in. (For example, some animals need access to outdoor space, so a high-rise flat would not be the best place for them to live.)

PERSPECTIVES

The Center for Animal Care and Control (CACC) is a not-for-profit organization that rescues, cares for and finds homes for homeless and abandoned animals in New York City in the USA.

'...we feel strongly that shelters are the best source for acquiring a pet. CACC evaluates all animals entering the system for both health and temperament. We ... make informed decisions about the appropriateness of an animal for specific circumstances. These may include homes with young children or other pets, or families who are away from the home for long hours each day. The CACC adoption staff cares deeply about the success of the placement, not the monetary value of a sale.'

The New York Center for Animal Care and Control website

Animal welfare supporters suggest that pet lovers should go to a rescue centre for their animals, rather than a breeder or a pet shop. With so many homeless animals in the world, they feel that it is important to give these unwanted pets a home, instead of encouraging breeders to breed even more animals. Although a number of these animals eventually find loving owners, many abandoned pets are still put down each year because there is no home to send them to.

Exotic pets

Cats, dogs, hamsters and gerbils have been domesticated so that they are suited to life with humans. Some people also keep exotic animals, such as monkeys, snakes and iguanas, as pets.

Many people believe that it is wrong for wild animals to be kept in surroundings that are totally unlike those they are used to. Also, as the needs of orangutans, gibbons and other wild animals are not as well known as those of domestic animals, they are more difficult to take care of. For instance, owners of exotic pets may fail to realize

A puppy waits for a new owner at a rescue centre.

PERSPECTIVES

People for the Ethical Treatment of Animals (PETA) is a US animal rights organization.

'In a perfect world, animals would be free… However, domesticated dogs and cats cannot survive "free" in our concrete jungles, so we must take as good care of them as possible. People with the time, money, love, and patience to make a lifetime commitment to an animal can make an enormous difference by adopting from shelters or rescuing animals from a perilous life on the street. But it is also important to stop manufacturing "pets", thereby perpetuating [continuing to breed] a class of animals forced to rely on humans to survive.'

PETA pamphlet, 'Companion Animals: Pets or Prisoners?'

how much it costs to recreate the surroundings, space and temperature of their pet's natural environment.

Campaigns by organizations such as WWF (originally the World Wildlife Fund and later the World Wide Fund for Nature) have brought about laws banning the sale of wild animals in some countries.

Selective breeding

When animals with the same characteristics – for example, height, weight or fur – reproduce, their offspring are likely to have the same characteristics. When humans breed animals in order to influence what they look like, or the way they behave, this is known as selective breeding. This has happened for thousands of years.

Selective breeding has created many different types of animal. For

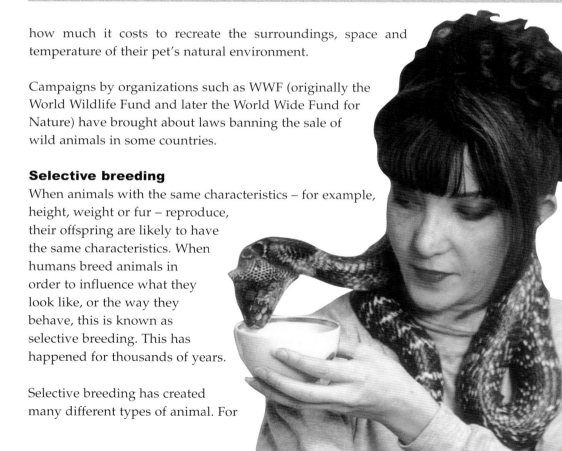

A woman with her pet cobra at her apartment in Moscow. Keeping exotic pets has become fashionable in Russia.

instance, greyhounds have been bred to chase animals at top speed, whereas terriers are small dogs, which have been bred to chase animals into small burrows and earths. Bulldogs were bred to irritate bulls in bull-baiting competitions hundreds of years ago.

However, the selective breeding of animals can cause health problems. For example, a bulldog's lower jawbone is longer than its upper jawbone, to enable the dog to keep a grip when it bites something. But the shape of a bulldog's head and nostrils means that they have breathing difficulties. Selective breeding can produce an animal that benefits humans, but does not necessarily benefit the animal.

A Beijing cat owner shows off her white cat – with one yellow and one blue eye. In China, different-coloured eyes are highly prized in this breed of long-haired cat. However, many of the cats are deaf as a result of the selective breeding used to achieve the odd eye colours.

DEBATE

Is it fair on animals to keep them as pets? What about domestic animals that have been bred to make good companions? Should these be returned to the wild? Would they be able to survive?

6: Animal Entertainment

Should animals be used to entertain humans? Is it acceptable that dolphins should jump through hoops to make a crowd gasp? Are zoos justified? Many people feel that all of these questions have the same answer – no. Other people enjoy watching dolphin displays and visiting zoos. Who is right?

The history of animal entertainment

Animals have been used to entertain humans for thousands of years. The Romans captured wild animals in North Africa and used them to entertain the crowds at the games in Rome. Later, in Britain, from the Middle Ages onwards, large audiences gathered to watch bear-baiting contests, where a chained bear would be attacked and tormented by fierce dogs.

Blood sports involve the hunting, wounding or killing of animals. Two examples are cock fighting and dog fighting, which were popular for many years and still take place in some parts of the world. These cruel 'sports' are watched by cheering crowds, who bet large sums of money on the outcome of a fight

A fourteenth-century illustration showing dogs being used to bait a bear.

PERSPECTIVES

The first dolphin show took place in Florida in 1938.

'The dolphin show does represent a form of education but it's a form of bad education in that it teaches millions of people that human supremacy over nature is a good thing.'

Helene O'Barry, The Dolphin Project website

that usually ends with the death of one animal. Both cock fighting and dog fighting are now banned in most parts of the world, although illegal fights still take place.

Many people enjoy watching other types of sport or entertainment involving animals, including bullfighting, horse racing, dog racing, dolphin displays, circus acts and zoos. All continue to arouse fierce debate.

Bullfighting

In Spain, Portugal and parts of southern France and Latin America, bullfighting has been popular since the early sixteenth century. Bulls bred to be savage and strong take part in a ceremonial fight with a matador (a human bullfighter). Tens of thousands of bulls are killed in bullfights every year and their deaths are rarely quick. In the bullring, the animals can be harpooned and tortured with flames, spears, swords and daggers. These facts enrage animal rights supporters around the world.

CASE STUDY

In the nineteenth and twentieth centuries, wild capuchin monkeys were tamed, then forced to walk upright and work for organ-grinders. While the street musician worked the barrel organ, the monkey collected money from onlookers.

In May 2001, the Jungle Friends Primate Sanctuary in Florida, USA, rescued Jimmy – a 40-year-old capuchin monkey. He had suffered years of abuse at the hands of an organ-grinder before being sold to a pet shop, where he was used to attract customers. Jimmy will now spend the rest of his life at the sanctuary with Chi Chi, an ex-circus monkey.

The Jungle Friends website, June 2003

PERSPECTIVES

The *Time Out* guide to Andalucía, in Spain, describes what takes place towards the end of a bullfight:

'If the matador is accurate and swift, there is little blood; the animal pauses and there is total silence in the ring; it sways slightly, staggers, its front legs give way and it collapses. However, if the kill is not clean, things can get very messy indeed; the bull will start staggering around, glassy-eyed, throwing up gallons of blood … while the matador either tries to finish the job himself with a … sword or instructs one of his men to stab the bull in the brain with a tiny dagger. Either way, it's horribly distressing to watch.'

Time Out: Andalucía *(Penguin, 2002)*

A bullfight in the Camargue region of France.

At the end of the twentieth century, 200,000 people – over 1 per cent of the Spanish workforce – were employed in the bullfighting industry. Those in favour of bullfighting argue that these jobs would be lost if the practice were banned. There are no signs of a total ban in the near future, but animal lovers have made some progress. The Spanish towns of Tossa de Mar, Vilamcolum and La Varjol have announced bullfighting bans, while the city of Jalapa in Mexico has also outlawed the 'sport'.

Circuses

The first time a circus performer appeared with wild animals was 1831. Since then, the circus ring has seen acts featuring many different animals, including lions, snakes, tigers, polar bears, giraffes, hippos, rhinos and – perhaps most famously – elephants.

Animal rights and welfare supporters argue that circus animals have usually been taken away from their natural habitat and that it is degrading for animals to entertain humans with tricks. There have also been cases of chimpanzees being beaten, and of whips and electric prods being used to force elephants and other wild animals to perform.

Although the number of circuses featuring animal acts has been dramatically reduced since the 1970s, many still exist. Protesters hope they will eventually disappear completely. In the meantime, an increasing number of animal-free circuses, featuring only human acts, are being formed. With these circuses, audiences continue to enjoy all the fun of the big top, without a single animal being involved.

Indian elephants performing in the Moscow State Circus in Russia.

PERSPECTIVES

The Society for the Prevention of Cruelty to Animals in British Columbia, Canada, would like the use of circus animals to be banned throughout the world.

'Most of a circus animal's life is spent travelling in cramped trucks... The only freedom and exercise they receive is while performing. Former animal trainers report observing or participating in abusive training practices such as beating or electroshocking bears, elephants, big cats and chimpanzees to force them to perform tricks. This is the price circus animals pay so that the public can have a few laughs.'

The Society for the Prevention of Cruelty to Animals in British Columbia website

PERSPECTIVES

Edinburgh Zoo, in Scotland, opened in 1913. It is one of the most famous zoos in the world.

'... [Our aim is] to inspire and excite our visitors with the wonder of living animals, and so to promote the conservation of threatened species and habitats ... we are involved in many conservation breeding programmes, and we give the highest priority to the welfare, both physical and behavioural, of the animals in our care.'

The Edinburgh Zoo website, June 2003

Zoos

Zoos keep wild animals in order to entertain the public, to study the animals, to educate people, to help conserve rare species, and – of course – many zoos are intended to make money. Each zoo may exist for some or all of these purposes.

Those opposed to zoos usually object to them because the animals live in captivity, instead of in their natural habitat. In the last century, animals were often kept behind bars or in concrete enclosures. Conditions are improving (zoos now attempt to imitate the conditions of an animal's home, although this can be very difficult to achieve in the smaller city zoos). The biggest zoos allow more room for animals to roam. Safari parks – where visitors can drive through the animals' natural habitat – allow animals to live in environments that are most like the wild.

Some zoo animals have been captured, while others have been born in captivity. When animals are captured, family groups are often broken up. Animal rights supporters feel that both ways of stocking zoos are wrong.

Those in favour of zoos argue that they allow scientists to observe wild animals' behaviour. Zoos allow animals in danger

A hippopotamus lies in its enclosure at the state-run zoo in Santiago, Chile, in 2001. Due to the poor conditions most of the animals were held in, the Chilean government invited local and international investors to bid for the construction of a new, privately run zoo.

of extinction to be bred in captivity, in order to keep a species alive. Finally, zoos mean that people can see animals from all over the world – no matter where they live.

Those against zoos feel that none of these reasons justify keeping wild animals in captivity.

Horses

The vast majority of horses in the world are domesticated. Some are kept as pets, some work for the police and on farms, while others take part in displays or sports that entertain humans. These include show jumping, horse racing, pony-and-trap racing, rodeo and polo. In each of these events, the horses have to obey humans' commands.

Some types of horse racing can be extremely dangerous for both horse and rider. In the Grand National, for instance, at Aintree in the north of England, 40 horses race around a dangerous track that includes towering jumps, but very few reach the finishing line. In 2003, only 14 horses completed the race, while one horse tragically died. Horse lovers and animal lovers worldwide have called for races of this type to be banned. They feel that horses should not be made to take part in a sport that could end in their death.

A steeplechase race in Saratoga Springs, New York, USA.

DEBATE

Are some forms of animal entertainment fairer to animals than others, or should they all be banned?

7: Endangered Species

In the twenty-first century, thousands of wild animal species are in danger of extinction. The greatest threats to their survival are hunting, loss of habitat, pollution and non-native animals. Do animals have the right to be protected from these dangers? Or are the needs of humans more important?

A nineteenth-century engraving of the dodo.

Hunted to extinction

During the last two thousand years, humans have done more to bring animal species to extinction than any other being on Earth. Some animals have been hunted to death. These include the dodo – a flightless bird that once lived on Mauritius (an island in the Indian Ocean). First spotted by Portuguese sailors in 1507, the dodo was probably extinct by 1683. In less than two hundred years every single dodo had been killed by humans, or by the animals these humans had introduced

PERSPECTIVES

Dr Annette Lanjouw, director of the International Gorilla Conservation Programme (IGCP), is pleased that numbers of endangered mountain gorillas in Uganda, Rwanda and the Democratic Republic of Congo have increased since 1989. Threats to the apes include hunting, capture for the illegal pet trade and habitat loss, especially due to war in the area.

'International and national efforts to protect this species have pulled the mountain gorilla back from the brink of extinction. However, if we want to ensure that they survive another hundred years, we must ensure that we lift the pressures that still threaten their forest home.'

The BBC news website, June 2003

to the dodo's natural habitat. The dodo, which had never seen any of these creatures before, failed to realize how dangerous they were and so was an easy target.

Organizations such as WWF and the World Conservation Union try to prevent animals becoming extinct. Many endangered species need their help, including the rhino. During the last two hundred years, rhino numbers have declined dramatically – from millions to just a few thousand. Half of the world's remaining rhinos disappeared during the 1970s. Rhino horn is used to make a traditional Chinese medicine that is said to cure fevers. As a result, poachers can sell the horns for huge amounts of money. The Convention on International Trade in Endangered Species (CITES) banned international trade in rhinos and their products in 1977. Park rangers now help to protect rhinos in Africa and Asia.

Animals are also taken from the wild to live as pets or to live in zoos (see pages 38 and 39). In other types of hunting, the animal is killed simply to provide a trophy for the hunter.

A black rhinoceros in Africa displays the horn which makes it the target of poachers. The world's rhino population has been decimated by poachers.

Animal habitat

The world's population is increasing. All over the planet, more land is being used to house and to feed people. Crops cover large areas, while towns are built in the middle of wild animals' territory. This means that many species, such as lions, elephants, pandas and chimpanzees, have less room to live and to find food. New roads can divide territories, making it difficult for rhinos and other species to find a mate.

For many species, well-managed wildlife reserves offer the best hope of survival. Reserves are protected areas where endangered species can live safely. The habitat is suited to the animals, there is enough space, and park rangers can protect them from poachers.

Pollution

Any change in the environment is bound to affect animals. However, man-made pollution – of air, sea and soil – is disastrous for animal species.

The *Exxon Valdez*, surrounded by the huge oil slick which devastated wildlife on the Alaskan coast in 1989.

CASE STUDY

The Orangutan Foundation International (OFI) is dedicated to the conservation of wild orangutans and their rainforest habitat in Indonesia and Malaysia.

In 1999, a young female orangutan was orphaned and made homeless by palm-oil plantation developers. Local villagers captured the orangutan and tied her up with wire cables. They were about to kill and sell her to the developers – who wanted to clear the area of this endangered species – when a passing truck driver saw what was happening and contacted OFI.

The young orangutan – named Ingrid – was rescued by OFI and taken to one of their care centres. When she had recovered from her ordeal, Ingrid was returned to the wild.

The Orangutan Foundation International website, June 2003

For example, pesticides and fertilizers do not only kill the pests at which they are aimed. The lesser horseshoe bat, found in parts of Europe, is just one victim of this form of pollution. This bat is becoming rarer because pesticides kill creatures that it eats.

Water pollution (waste pumped into rivers and seas) affects many animals. If the sea is polluted, smaller creatures are poisoned. When larger animals, such as dolphins and sharks, eat these creatures, they become ill themselves.

Environmental disasters can devastate wildlife. For instance, the oil spilled by the *Exxon Valdez* tanker in 1989 ruined 2,400 kilometres of Alaskan coastline and wiped out huge numbers of birds and fish. Oil coated the birds' feathers, making it difficult for them to fly, and fish were poisoned. It took years for the area to recover.

There is also the problem of global warming. When people burn fossil fuels – such as oil and coal – carbon dioxide and other gases are released into the air. These gases trap energy from the sun, creating the greenhouse effect (or global warming) which is slowly melting the ice in the Arctic and Antarctic. The penguin is one species whose territory is shrinking as the ice melts. Countries around the world are reducing the pollution that is pumped into the atmosphere, but it remains to be seen whether this will slow down global warming.

A melting glacier at Qaanaaq, in north-west Greenland.

Non-native animals

Humans have been exploring different parts of the world for thousands of years. However, when people moved to new areas they took animals with them. Sometimes, these imported creatures had a harmful effect on their new environment.

For instance, when rabbits were taken to Australia in the late nineteenth century, no one realized just how quickly they would breed. The rabbits escaped into the wild, soon covering the entire

A pair of giant pandas, on loan from the China Research and Conservation Centre, feeding at Washington National Zoo, USA, in 2002.

PERSPECTIVES

In 1998, the Pennsylvania 21st Century Environment Commission's report on conserving natural resources was published.

'Plants, animals, fungi and micro-organisms … in combination weave the web that holds together … all life on Earth. The quality and strength of the web is dependent on the quality of our natural support systems – water, land and air… The diversity of life is a key measure of the health of our environment now and of its future reliability … for humans.'

The Pennsylvania 21st Century Environment Commission website

PERSPECTIVES

According to WWF, an international charity:

'The need to reduce and repair habitat loss, to cut down on our reliance on persistent chemicals, to combat global warming, prevent the introduction of alien species, stop the illegal trade in animal parts ... it is all within our power to stop and reverse the destructive trends that we see. From what we buy in the shops, to what we say and read, who we vote for, and what we campaign for – this is where the pressure must come from if governments, business, and industry are to make the changes that will ultimately conserve life on earth.'

The WWF website

continent, grazing in areas where native animals lived, and leaving little food for the Australian wildlife. Rabbits may have contributed to the extinction of many native Australian plant and animal species. The controversial introduction of a deadly rabbit disease called myxomatosis in the 1950s did little to reduce the numbers. Rabbits remain Australia's most serious animal pest.

Helping animals to survive

Organizations around the world have been campaigning to save endangered species from extinction for years:

• by creating public awareness about habitat destruction, environmental problems and why animals are in danger

• by working with governments and local communities to develop strategies for dealing with these problems

• and by helping local people to understand that their standard of living is dependent on conserving the environment, both local and global.

WWF and other like-minded organizations feel that it is not a question of putting human rights or animal rights first. Conservation of the environment will help humans and animals to survive side by side in the future.

DEBATE

Should the panda be given more publicity than the fragile tree snail? Are cute, cuddly mammals entitled to more protection than slimy molluscs? How should organizations that support conservation decide how to spend their money?

Glossary

activist a person who campaigns vigorously to bring about change.

anaesthesia drugs or gases used before an operation to make a patient unconscious, so that they do not feel pain.

antibiotic medicine that kills micro-organisms.

by-product something that is made when another product is created.

cloning creating genetically identical cells or living things.

cohesive when something holds things together.

conservation keeping or restoring the environment and wildlife.

crustacea creatures such as crabs, lobsters and shrimps.

diphtheria a deadly disease that causes swelling of the thoat.

dissection cutting up a body or a plant in order to study it.

distemper a disease that causes fever and coughing in animals.

ecosystem all the plants and animals in a particular environment, e.g. a pond, a forest or a whole planet.

electroshocking applying electric shocks to the brain.

exploitation when something is used unfairly.

extinction when every single animal or plant of a particular species dies.

farrier a person, usually a blacksmith, who makes shoes for horses.

fertilizer waste matter or chemical used to make soil more fertile, so plants grow more quickly.

free-range kept in a natural environment where it is possible to move freely.

gelatine a see-through material, made from animal tissue, used to prepare some types of food, such as jelly.

gene tiny information-carrying cell passed on from parent to offspring.

habitat place where a human or animal lives.

humane when a process is as painless and as kind to the animal concerned as possible.

immune system the tissues and cells that defend the body against infection.

micro-organisms a very small living thing, such as a bacterium, virus or fungus.

organic produced without using chemicals.

pesticide waste matter or chemical used to kill animal or plant pests.

polio an infectious disease that can cause paralysis.

quarry an animal that is being hunted.

rennet curdled milk, from the stomach of a young calf, used to make cheese.

smallpox a deadly disease that causes fever.

species a group of living things.

sterilization when a creature's ability to have offspring is stopped.

tetanus a serious disease that makes muscles go rigid or into spasm.

tuberculosis an infectious disease that causes growths in the lungs.

ultrasound scanning a modern medical technique for taking a picture of the inside of a body using sound or vibration.

vaccine medicine that helps prevent disease.

vivisection the practice of performing operations on live animals for the purpose of scientific research.

Useful Addresses

http://www.petakids.com/index.html
PETA (People for the Ethical Treatment of Animals) website for children
'The world's largest animal rights organization's website for kids who care.'

http://www.yptenc.org.uk
YPTE Young People's Trust for the Environment

http://www.aspca.org
ASPCA (American Society for the Prevention of Cruelty to Animals)

http://www.rspca.org.uk
RSPCA (Royal Society for the Prevention of Cruelty to Animals)

http://www.wwf.org/
WWF, the global environment network

http://www.fawc.org.uk/freedoms.htm
Farm Animal Welfare Council – the five freedoms

http://www.friendsofanimals.org
Friends of Animals

http://www.exzooberance.com
Exzooberance – celebrating the animal kingdom!

http://www.ciwf.co.uk
CIWF (Compassion in World Farming)

Further Reading

Talking Points: Animal Rights
Barbara James
(Hodder Wayland, 2002)

The Young Person's Guide to Animal Rights
Barbara James
(Virago Press, 1992)

For older readers

Animal Rights and Wrongs
Roger Scruton
(Metro Books, 2000)

Animal Rights – A Very Short Introduction
David DeGrazia
(Oxford University Press, 2002)

Animal Underworld: Inside America's Black Market for Rare and Exotic Species
Alan Green
(Public Affairs, 1999)

Animal Welfare (Earth at Risk)
Julie Catalano
(Chelsea House Publishers, 1995)

The Livewire Guide to Going, Being and Staying Veggie!
Juliet Gellatley
(Livewire Books for Teenagers, 1996)

Index

Numbers in **bold** refer to pictures.

animal rescue centres 30, 31, **31**
animal research 4, 11, 20, **20**, 21, 22, 23, **23**, 24, 25, 26, 27
apes 40, 42

bats 43
bears 34, **34**
birds 43
blood sports 34, **34**
breeding, selective 32, 33, **33**
BSE 9
bullfighting 35, 36, **36**

cats **25**, 28, 30, 31, 32, 33
circuses 35, 36, 37, **37**
clay-pigeon shooting 17, **17**
cock fighting 34
conservation 38, 39, 41, 45
cows 8, **10**, 26
culling 16, 17

deer 4, **14**, 15, 16, **16**
dodos 40, **40**
dogs **14**, 16, 18, 25, 28, 29, **29**, 30, 31, **31**, 32, 33, 34, **34**
dolphins 4, 12, 13, 34, 35, 43
drag hunting 18
drift net fishing 12, 13
ducks **8**, 9

elephants 18, 37, **37**, 42
endangered species 26, 40, 41, **41**, 42, 43, 44, **44**, 45
exotic pets 31, 32, **32**

factory farming 9
farm animals 4, **5**, 6, **6**, 7, **7**, 8, 9, 10, **10**, 12, **12**, 13, 14, 39

fish 10, 11, **11**, 12, **12**, 30, **30**, 43
'five freedoms' 4
foot-and-mouth disease 9
foxes 16, 17, 19
fur industry 18, 19, **19**

geese **8**, 9
genetic engineering 22, 23, **23**
gerbils 31
global warming 43, **43**
goldfish 30, **30**

habitat, loss of 40, 41, 42, 45
hamsters **28**, 30, 31
hens 6, **6**, 7, **7**
hippopotamuses **38**
horses 30, 35, 39, **39**
humane sports 17, **17**, 18
hunting 14, **14**, 15, 16, **16**, 17, 40

insects 4

LD50 test 27
lions 28, 36, 42

medical advances 21, **21**, 22, 23, 25, 26, **26**, 27
mice 17, **20**, 27, 29
monkeys 28, 31, 35

non-native animals 40, 41, 44, 45

organic farming 9

pandas 42, **44**, 45
penguins 43
pets 4, 28, **28**, 29, **29**, 30, **30**, 31, 32, **32**, 33, **33**, 39, 41
pigs 20
poaching 18, 41
pollution 40, 42, **42**, 43

porpoises **11**, 13

rabbits 27, 28, 30, 44, 45
Regan, Tom 4
rhinoceroses 41, **41**, 42
Ryder, Richard 4, 5

safari parks 38
salmon 12, **12**
seals 15
sheep **5**
Singer, Peter 4, 5
snakes 31, **32**
speciesism 5

'three Rs' 26

veal 8
vegetarians 13, 15
veterinary treatment 25, **25**, 26, 27, 29, 30
vivisection 24, 25

wildlife reserves 42

zoos 34, 38, **38**, 39, 41